Mia and Anthony and the Hidden Treasures

Treasure Number Four –
Making Money Grow!

About the Author

Joe Khoury writes on topics that are important to him; on core values that he hopes would inspire, educate and enlighten his children, step-children and hopefully others.

In 2019 he found a few precious notes in his mother's handwriting; Having lost both his parents while so young, he realized that he didn't really know much about them: what were their likes, dislikes, hopes, fears and even points of view on certain topics? He decided to begin writing so that – in the event that something should happen to him, my children and even future grandchildren would be able to know the core values and life lessons he hopes for them to learn.

Learn more about the author and the characters by visiting our website at
lessonsformykidsbooks.com
or scan the QR Code below

"Dad! Mom!" shouted Anthony, rushing towards his parents. "I've had a brilliant idea!"

"No, you haven't!" said Mia, running after him. "It was my idea!"

"Well, let's hear this wonderful idea," laughed Dad.

"We want skateboards," said Anthony.

"Yes, they're so much fun," said Mia.

"Well," said Dad. "Of course, you can have skateboards…"

"Hurrah!" shouted the twins, jumping up and down with excitement.

"Wait, I haven't finished," said Dad. "You see, there's something we need to talk about."

"Do you mean what color skateboard to get?" asked Anthony.

"No," said Dad. "We need to think about how you will pay for them."

"What do you mean, Dad?" asked Mia.

"Well, we get things we need from stores – everything from skateboards to clothes and the food we eat. When we buy these things, we have to give money to the storekeeper."

"Oh!" said Mia. "I haven't any money."

"Neither have I," added Anthony. "How can we get some?"

"Well," said Dad. "How do I get money?"

"By going to work," said Anthony.

"That's right. So, why don't you work to earn money for the skateboards?"

"That's a great idea, Dad," said Anthony. "I'm going to be an astronaut or a police officer or the captain of a great, big ship."

"I'm going to be a doctor," said Mia, "Or perhaps a teacher or a vet." Dad and Mom both laughed.

"Those are exciting choices," said Mom, "But you're a little too young for those jobs. Our neighbor, Louise, needs some help, though. Let's go and see her."

Louise was very happy when the twins offered to help. Their first job was helping to plant some flowers. They had to dig a row of small holes and drop the little seeds in them.

"These flower seeds are tiny," said Mia.

"Yes," replied Louise. "But if we look after them, they'll grow and grow. Soon, they'll be big, bright flowers."

It was a tricky job but great fun. When they finished, Louise gave them five dollars each.

Anthony and Mia rushed home and showed the money to Mom and Dad.

"Can we buy some candy?" asked Anthony.

"I'm afraid not," said Dad. "Skateboards cost more than five dollars, so you need to save your money."

"What does that mean?" asked Mia.

"It means looking after your money until you have enough to buy the skateboards."

"Oh," said Anthony. "You mean that, if we look after the dollars, they'll grow and grow just like the flower seeds."

So, that's exactly what they did. Their next job was sweeping Louise's driveaway. They took a broom from home and some bags to put the rubbish in. Soon, the driveway looked wonderful. Louise gave them a great big smile and another five-dollar bill.

The twins were very good workers and very good at saving. Next, they raked the leaves in Louise's garden and filled lots of bags with all the brown leaves. Then, they looked after Louise's cat when she went away for a few days. This was their favorite job and they fed the little cat every morning and every evening. They didn't forget once.

The more jobs they did, the more their money grew. They washed Louise's car, helped paint her fence and even mowed the lawn.

It was soon time to count their savings to see if they had enough money.

"Look how much money we have now, Dad!" said Mia.

"Yes, but you need to give me five dollars," said Dad. He reached over a took a five- dollar bill from their money.

"Hey!" shouted Anthony. "That's ours! Give it back!"

"But I need the money to buy more bags," said Dad. "You used lots of them when you cleaned Louise's driveway and garden."

"That's not fair!" said Anthony. "Nobody takes away your money."

"Oh, yes, they do," replied Dad. "How do you think the Government pays for all those nice schools?"

"Er... I don't know," said Anthony.

"And how does it find the money to build the roads we drive along?" asked Dad.

Anthony and Mia looked at each other. They'd never thought about that.

"And how do they pay for fire trucks? Or street lights? Or all the other things we need?" Dad smiled at the twins. They looked very confused.

"Well," said Dad. "We all need these things, so we all pay for them. The Government takes some money from everybody. This is called tax."

"I see," said Mia. "So, you're taking some tax from us to buy more bags. That's fair."

"Yes," said Dad. "Anyway, let's go and buy your skateboards."

Just then, Jillian came in. Anthony smiled at her.

"We're going to buy our skateboards, today," he said to his big sister. "Do you want to come?"

"Yes, please," said Jillian and they all rushed to the car.

The twins ran into the toy store. There were lots of skateboards hanging on the walls.

There were blue ones, red ones and yellow ones. There were fat ones and slim ones. There were skateboards with red wheels, black wheels, even green wheels.

"What about those, Mia?" said Anthony pointing at a pair of bright red skateboards with yellow flames painted on them.

"They're fantastic! Can we have those, Dad?"

"Well," answered Dad. "You have 45 dollars each, but they cost 55 dollars."

"Can we borrow another 10 dollars each, Dad. Then, we can buy them."

"I'm not sure that's a good idea," said Dad. "It costs money to borrow money. If the bank leant me 10 dollars, they might make me pay 12 dollars back."

"Wow! That's not fair!" said Mia. "Let's buy different skateboards… ones we can afford."

The twins soon found the perfect skateboards. They were blue with white lightning flashes on them. They looked really cool and they only cost 25 dollars.

"These are beautiful, Mia!", said Anthony.

"Yes," said Mia. "And we have 20 dollars each left. We can buy an awful lot of candy."

"I don't think so," said Dad slowly.

"Why not?" asked Anthony.

"Well, do you remember Louise's tiny flower seeds?" asked Dad. "If she looks after them, they'll grow and grow."

"Money is confusing," said Anthony. "Are you saying we should plant our money in the ground?"

"No," smiled Dad. "But there is somewhere you can plant it and watch it grow. Come on! I'll show you."

So, off they went to the bank and opened a savings account. Every time they earned money they could put some of it in here and their savings would grow and grow. The bank would even add a little more to their savings.

"Just think," said Dad. "When we go on vacation, you can use some of your savings. That way, you'll have money to spend."

"Let's put all our money in!" said Mia. "We have 20 dollars each."

"Why not just put 10 dollars in?" suggested Dad. "Later, I'll show you something else you can do with the rest of your money."

The twins agreed. They were pleased Dad was teaching them about money. Next, Dad turned to Jillian.

"While we're talking about money, Jillian, let's open your investing account."

"Is that the same as our savings account?" asked Anthony.

"Sort of," said Dad. "It's another place to put your money and watch it grow. Actually, it can help your money grow even more quickly."

"Wow! As quickly as the beanstalk in Jack and the Beanstalk?" asked Mia.

"Not quite that fast," laughed Dad. "But it can be a little bit risky, like the beanstalk. A giant won't come and get you but there is a chance your money could shrink instead of grow."

"Why?" asked Anthony.

"Well, there are lots of businesses in America. It was a business that made your skateboard in a factory. Another business sold it in the shop. Businesses like these need money to build factories and shops and pay people to work for them. When you put your money in an investing account, you are buying part of these businesses. If they grow, your money grows."

"Are you going to put Jillian's money in the skateboard business?" asked Mia.

"No," said Dad. "I don't know which businesses to choose. So, I'll give the money to an organization called Vanguard. They will spread Jillian's money among some good businesses for me. This is called an index fund."

"Hurrah! You'll be rich soon, Jillian!" Anthony smiled at his big sister.

"I don't think so," said Jillian. "I'm going to leave the money there for a long time. I'll keep adding more money, as well."

As soon as the twins got home, they went out on their skateboards. It was tricky learning how to balance. Soon, though, they were zooming up and down the sidewalk. When they went in for dinner, Anthony suddenly remembered something.

"Dad," he said. "We made 50 dollars and gave you 5 dollars in tax. Then we spent 25 dollars on the skateboards and put 10 dollars into a savings account."

"That's right," said Dad.

"That means we still have 10 dollars each," said Mia.

"That's right," said Dad.

"We're really pleased you worked so hard to buy your lovely skateboards," said Mom. "But not everyone can make money like that."

"No," said Dad. "Some people live in very poor countries."

"And some people are too sick to work," said Mom.

"Can we use our 10 dollars to help them?" asked Mia.

"That's a great idea," said Anthony.

Mia decided to give her ten dollars to help bring clean water to a poor African village. Anthony gave his to buy medicine for war veterans in America. They were so happy and they promised to give money to help other people every year.

Finally, after a long day of shopping and skateboarding, it was time for bed.

"I love our new skateboards, Anthony," said Mia, yawning. She was very tired.

"Yes," said Anthony, "And we've learned so much today."

"I know," said Mia. "If we work hard and look after our money, we'll be able to buy the things we want, save up and help other people, as well."

"Goodnight, Mia," said Anthony. "Let's go to sleep. Tomorrow, we'll wake up early and play on our skateboards all day."

What have we learned?

- Money is something that we use to buy things like food, clothes, toys and more.
- We earn money by going to work.
- The government takes a portion of the money we earn to build schools and roads and pay the fire fighters and police. This is called "tax".
- We should not spend all the money we earn:
- A portion of it should go into the bank in what we call a "savings account". This is a safe place where you save money for future purchases or emergencies.
- Another portion should go into "investing": This is where your money can grow and make more money.
- One last portion will go into helping poor people.
- The rest is all yours to spend on something fun!

Now go make the world a better place!

www.ingramcontent.com/pod-product-compliance
Lightning Source LLC
Chambersburg PA
CBHW040109120526
44589CB00040B/2831